MW00678372

101 Things to Do in
GEORGIA
Before You Up and Die

SWEET
WATER
PRESS

101 Things to Do in Georgia
Copyright © 2006 Sweetwater Press
Produced by Cliff Road Books

ISBN: 1-58173-558-8
ISBN-13: 9781581735581

Researched and co-written by Holly Smith
Jacket and text design by Miles G. Parsons
Printed in Italy

1. Pick a peach.

2. Sleep in a hammock on a screened porch.

3. Get stuck in traffic on I-285.

4. Have a burger and shake at The Varsity.

5. Go Underground Atlanta.

6. Tour the Braves Hall of Fame at Turner Field.

7. Go to the practice
rounds of
The Masters.

8. Watch UGA and Georgia Tech fight for braggin' rights.

9. Stroll down River Street in Savannah.

10. See the dancing water show at Centennial Olympic Park.

11. Float down the Chattahoochee River.

12. See a UFO in LaGrange.

13. Test your fear
of heights on
Acrophobia at
Six Flags.

14. Stay at a haunted B & B.

15. Pat Uga.

16. Taste all the
international
versions of
Coca-Cola.

17. Tour the Pebble
Hill Plantation in
Thomasville.

✓18. Take a ghost
tour of Savannah.

19. See the wild horses on Cumberland Island.

20. Hike the Appalachian Trail.

21. Master the recipe for cheese grits.

22. Go to church with Jimmy Carter.

23. Have your picture taken at the top of Peachtree Tower.

24. Picnic at Piedmont Park.

25. Polka at Oktoberfest in Helen.

26. Hear the Atlanta Symphony.

27. Spend your paycheck shopping in Buckhead.

28. See the Georgia Music Hall of Fame.

29. Drink sweet tea and rock on the porch all day.

30. Take a horse-drawn carriage tour of Jekyll Island.

31. Visit Callaway Gardens when the azaleas are blooming.

32. Cross the Swing-A-Long Bridge in Rock City.

33. See the generals at Stone Mountain.

34. Backpack to Amicalola Falls.

35. Kayak through Tallulah Gorge.

36. Try the fried apple pie and cider at Mercier Orchards.

37. Count the number of streets in Atlanta named Peachtree.

38. Celebrate Gold Rush Days in Dahlonega.

39. Hang glide off Lookout Mountain.

40. Tailgate at Atlanta Motor Speedway.

41. Eat boiled peanuts in Plains.

42. Trace Sherman's "March to the Sea" by car.

43. Whitewater raft the Chattooga.

44. See a polo match at the Georgia International Horse Park.

45. Go skydiving.

46. Tour CNN.

47. See how many things you can make with Vidalias.

48. Visit the State Botanical Garden in every season.

49. Go deep-sea fishing.

✓ 50. Take a dolphin cruise.

✓ 51. See every square in Savannah.

52. Browse the
Antiques Trail.

53. Waterski on
Lake Lanier.

54. Visit the Martin Luther King Library.

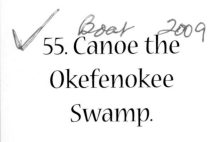

✓ Boat 2009

55. Canoe the
Okefenokee
Swamp.

56. Go birdwatching on Sea Island.

57. Climb the Native American mounds in Macon.

58. Explore Cave Springs.

59. Walk across the Euharlee Covered Bridge.

60. Say a prayer at Chickamauga.

61. Go camping at Fort Yargo.

✓ 62. Meet Ted Turner.

63. Climb to the top of the Tybee Island lighthouse.

64. Have a fish fry.

65. Ride the ferry to Sapelo Island.

66. See Providence Canyon in autumn.

67. Make par.

68. Boogie all night in Athens.

69. Tour Flannery O'Connor's farm.

70. Go sea kayaking.

71. See the
<u>Unfinished Portrait</u>
of FDR in
Warm Springs.

72. Rent a cabin in the Blue Ridge Mountains.

73. Read <u>Gone with the Wind</u>. R 2012

74. Call someone "hon."

75. Look a whale shark in the eye at the Atlanta Aquarium.

76. Go to the Dekalb Farmers Market.

77. Eat at The Lady and Sons.

78. See the Hawks and Thrashers play at Philips Arena.

79. Ring in the new year at the Peach Drop.

80. Go to the High Museum.

81. Go to a concert at The Tabernacle.

82. Feel sorry for someone who doesn't live in Georgia.

83. Plant a dogwood tree.

84. Cheer on the cyclists in the Tour de Georgia.

85. Save a sea turtle.

86. Drink a mint julep.

87. Listen to jazz on the St. Simon's lighthouse lawn.

88. Pick pumpkins at a pumpkin patch.

89. Get lost in a corn maze.

90. Walk among the dinosaurs at Fernbank.

91. Learn the back roads around the Bypass.

92. Relive the Battle of Atlanta at the Cyclorama.

✓ 93. Watch a Civil War reenactment.

94. Devour a slab
of ribs.

95. Go fly fishing.

96. Learn to make mayonnaise.

97. Touch a snake.

98. Watch a production of <u>Swamp Gravy</u> in Colquitt.

99. Celebrate the National Grits Festival.

100. Try playing the banjo.

101. Stand under a magnolia and be glad. You're in Georgia!